LOVING

⁓∞⁓

EACH
DAY

REFLECTIONS ON THE
*S*PIRIT WITHIN

BOOKS BY JOHN-ROGER

Awakening Into Light
Baraka
Blessings of Light
The Buddha Consciousness
*The Christ Within & The Disciples of Christ with the
    Cosmic Christ Calendar*
The Consciousness of Soul
A Consciousness of Wealth
Dream Voyages
Drugs
Dynamics of the Lower Self
Forgiveness: The Key to the Kingdom
God Is Your Partner
Inner Worlds of Meditation
Journey of a Soul
Manual on Using the Light
The Master Chohans of the Color Rays
Passage Into Spirit
The Path to Mastership
Possessions, Projections, & Entities
The Power Within You
Psychic Protection

Q & A Journal from the Heart
Relationships—The Art of Making Life Work
Sex, Spirit, & You
The Signs of the Times
The Sound Current
The Spiritual Family
The Spiritual Promise
Spiritual Warrior: The Art of Spiritual Living
The Tao of Spirit
Walking with the Lord
The Way Out Book
Wealth & Higher Consciousness

For Further Information, Please Contact:

MSIA®
P.O. Box 513935
Los Angeles, CA 90051-1935
323-737-4055
soul@msia.org
www.msia.org

LOVING

EACH
DAY

REFLECTIONS ON THE
SPIRIT WITHIN

JOHN-ROGER

MANDEVILLE PRESS
Los Angeles, Califonia

Published by Mandeville Press
P.O. Box 513935
Los Angeles, CA 90051-1935
323-737-4055
jrbooks@msia.org
www.mandevillepress.org

Printed in the United States of America
ISBN 0-914829-26-2

INTRODUCTION

IN THE EARLY 1980's a small printing of a little book was released. It did not make a big splash, but it did make a big impression. Though it sold out fairly quickly, there were no plans to reprint it. However, over time, demand for the book would not go away. In fact, instead of fading, it increased.

With the expansion of the Internet, the idea behind the book was taken and presented in the form of a daily, free, subscriber-only e-mail named after the book. Though it became extremely popular, it did not replace the desire for the book. If anything, it increased it.

And so, this wonderful little book, *Loving Each Day*, was reprinted.

Loving Each Day is one of those gems that can be used for upliftment and inspiration in endless ways. Keep it by your bedside and open it at random when you awaken to find a theme for the day. Or read a quote just before turning out the light at night. Put it on the coffee table for a quick jolt of inspiration whenever you or guests need it, or read a page a day just for the pleasure of it.

However you use this book, you are sure to find joy and happiness transmitted from its pages into your heart.

*I*f you would learn the secret of Soul

Transcendence, look only for the good,

for the Divine in people and things, and all

the rest leave to God.

*T*his new age of living love manifests
each time you enter into the love of the
spiritual heart.

*T*he message of the age is that God's love is manifest here and now, within every one.

*W*hen you see the positive in all things,

when you are of service to yourself and others,

when you work always to lift yourself and others,

you are living love.

*T*he energy of living love can give courage
and hope; it can renew the faith of everyone
around you. Find that center of living love,
and give from that level.

*A*s you reach into your heart and manifest love, you have fulfilled all the laws, all the prophecies, and all the scriptures. You have manifested your divinity for all to see.

$\mathcal{W}$hen you awaken to your own Christ consciousness, to your own Soul consciousness, you will love freely, you will live freely, you will love from the loving heart. You will be living love.

*Y*ou have to actively place yourself in a position to receive what you want.

When you are in a state of cooperation,
your attitude is one of joy, enthusiasm,
and abundance.

*C*omplete the projects you begin, fulfill the commitments you have made, live up to the promises you have made.

Set your goals high and go for them. Don't let anyone or anything sidetrack you. Create only the very best things for yourself.

*Y*ou bring to yourself that which you focus
upon, so it makes sense to focus on the best,
the highest thing you know.

It is important to take responsibility for your actions. It becomes more and more difficult to lay your troubles at somebody else's doorstep and say, "My misery is your fault." No, your misery is only your choice. Your joy is also your choice.

$\mathcal{L}$ove will take care of you. Love is the guiding

Light inside of you. Pure love is the Soul.

*T*here will come a time when you will receive the divine Light and know it in your consciousness. You will receive your own awakening and say, "I am already that of which you speak. I am the love of which you speak."

*M*anifest loving in all you do. When you work, work in loving. When you play, play in loving. When you touch someone, touch with loving. And when you speak, speak with loving, for love is the sound of the Soul.

*T*hat twinkle in the eye, that smile on the face, that awareness that says, "I know you're here; I can see you"—that's living love!

As long as you focus on the outer world, you see imbalance and dis-ease. There is no need to reside in that; there is a place inside of you wherein resides serenity.

*G*od speaks to those who live in the spiritual heart. Create words of harmony and love. Create thoughts that are worthy of the divinity within you. Create loving that can be manifested anywhere, at any time. Walk with the Beloved and just be one with all.

*W*hen you get high enough in the consciousness of God, everyone has the same name. That name is *love*.

$\mathcal{P}$ractice finding the living love within you

before looking outward.

$\mathcal{Y}$ou can break free of limitations by sacrificing

every one of them.

*W*hen you are free, you do not have to demonstrate it.

$\mathcal{T}$ake care of yourself, so you can help take

care of others.

We are all our brothers' keepers, but not as prison keepers. We keep our brothers free by allowing them the individual experience of their own life, the way they see it.

*T*rue freedom is expressing yourself freely and

allowing others that same freedom.

$\mathcal{D}$isturbing action creates karma. Disturbing reaction perpetrates karma. When you change disturbing action to loving action, and disturbing reaction to acceptance and understanding, you may experience love, joy, peace, and fulfillment. These divine attributes help maintain the harmony of God's creation.

*I*n the total consciousness of One, you realize that this body is all the bodies, that this heart is all the hearts, that this love is all the loves, that this God is all the Gods, and in that, we have our living and our breathing, our coming in and going out, our death and our resurrection.

God has given us life—the most precious

of all commodities—and then said,

"Do what you will."

Life is awareness. Life is love.

$\mathcal{T}$here is only one reality: that which is the heart, that which is the Soul, that which is God, that which *is*.

*E*verybody's going to make it into the

high consciousness of God by way

of the spiritual heart.

*I*n the Christ resides spiritual protection.

And Christ resides in your spiritual heart.

*Y*our body is a temple, on this level, for the consciousness that is the most high.

*G*od is living love. To go to God, you must also be living love; and then you are also God.

You cannot be divorced or separated from that

which you truly are.

$\mathcal{T}$ruth is within you. God is within you.

Love is within you.

When you look to the spiritual heart for your fulfillment, when you become pure of heart, when you let the spiritual heart speak, when you love—then the body, mind, and emotions follow and you express total loving.

Get busy now and do those things that will bring you the honor and glory that is yours.

*E*veryday we create anew by flowing with

what is present.

*P*art of your job is to create the most perfect environment for yourself and for others when they come into your presence.

Living love cannot hurt, harm, or hamper.

Living love lifts.

When you give from the consciousness of living love and service, you will receive all that you give—and more—in return.

$\mathcal{E}$verything is now. This is the moment of
God's eternity—right now. It goes into the past
and into the future, but it is all now.
There is no place that you can think or be that
you are not within eternity.

*H*ome is where the Spirit of Christ reigns eternally and that is in the spiritual heart.

$\mathcal{W}$here there is love, there you have

found home.

You reside, always, in the heart of God.

God is the perfect lover. All else is imperfect, and yet is perfect because it is part of God. Some part is always perfect, some thought is always magnificent, some deed is always charitable.

$\mathcal{W}$hen you bring yourself into a loving consciousness with all things, peace and harmony will enfold your heart, and you will recognize within every level of your beingness that there is only love.

*G*ive from the spiritual heart and you'll be amazed at how Spirit takes care of its own.

*I*t's a challenge to take that which has been your hurt, your anger, your grief, and use these as stepping stones to go higher in your spiritual freedom.

*A*s God in manifestation, you are
responsible for what you create.

The Soul attracts to itself the positive essence: truth, love, joy, peace, and fulfillment.

*N*egative expressions that disturb creation are re-cycled by the law of cause and effect, action and reaction, until the consciousness is balanced through acceptance and understanding.

You experience love to become love.

You experience Light to become Light.

You must be child-like to enter into the

kingdom of heaven.

$\mathcal{T}$he value of each experience is in the

understanding and growing.

*L*et your love be your guiding star. Let it be your breath. Then you live in the heart of God. All things are made new, and God is personally present, all the time.

$\mathcal{T}$he Soul is life and gives health. Even though
the mental, emotional, and physical bodies may
suffer from negativity, hurt and disease,
the Soul can continually revive them
and bring forth healing.

$\int$pirit presents to you infinite opportunity.

*Y*our prime direction is to understand your own

beingness. That's a full-time job.

$\mathcal{B}$e devoted to yourself.

*L*ook within yourself, inquire within yourself

to find understanding.

*Y*our own inner counselor is your revelator.

Living love is not just loving from someplace deep within you, but living love with every breath. When you breathe in, love breathes in. And when you breathe out, love breathes out.

*E*ach heart awakens a little more as

it trusts itself.

*T*hose people who are fortunate enough to experience love are, indeed, saintly people. Those people who are fortunate enough to express love are the avatars of the ages.

$\mathcal{W}$hen you are loving, you have the consciousness of self present.

God is the instigator; the Traveler is the sender; Hu-man is the receiver; the Christ within is the decider; and you, consciously, are the completer.

*I*gnorance is a sin—the only sin. When you come into understanding, ignorance drops away and you change automatically.

*U*nconditionally love all things.

When you feel like you'd like to give
someone a piece of your mind, give them,
instead, a piece of your heart; give them love.

*T*he Beloved stands with you and gives
love to you.

You are divine love. You are living love.

*A*lways use love all ways.

*T*here is only one mind, and that is the
mind of God. There is only one love,
and that is the love of God.

$\mathcal{W}$hen you speak of God,

you attune yourself to God.

*D*ig deeply into the spring of love and partake of it. The supply is infinite.

*A*nyone who is residing in the power of
love is never destroyed, never separated,
always free, always up, always growing.

*L*ove is living in the spiritual heart.

When you come to the spiritual heart, you
find yourself in the center of all beingness.
At that point, you reside at the apex of time
and all things are delivered unto you.

When you become one with life, the very leaves on the trees are the scripture of nature. The face you look at is the scripture of your own beingness. The aura around you is the scripture of your mind and emotions, and very often, of your own spirituality. The very Soul is seeing the face of God in the physical world.

*G*od sees only perfection.

*G*od may be many different sizes, shapes
and forms. But it is all God. It is all divine
love made manifest.

*G*od loves all of its creation.

*I*f you strive for perfection, the work you have

started will be finished by the Christ.

*A*s you exercise freedom, you learn to be responsible for what you create and thus are educated by your own experience.

*I*t is your choice to determine the level

of your experience.

$\mathcal{Y}$ou will never be given anything you

can't handle.

*I*f something appears to be a block, then it can
be a stepping stone. All the force that is pulling
against you can be changed to lift you.

*T*he only way to grow is to grow. It's easier on you if you choose to grow willingly, knowingly, with acceptance, enthusiasm, understanding, and cooperation.

*I*f you don't learn something every day,

what are you doing, anyway?

You must be the teacher of the level
below you, a competent worker on the
level you're on, and a student on the level
above you; then you can move ahead in
your spiritual consciousness.

Can you truthfully say, "I am the Light, the Truth, the Way"? If you do not say that, you do not say a truth at all.

*P*ut the Light around the world.
Ask to live each moment in the consciousness
of the Light, and to be the Light.

$\mathcal{W}$hen you do the Father's work,

you do everything perfectly.

*T*he willingness to do creates the ability to do.

If you look deeply into people, you will

see something very majestic.

*D*ivine love is given to everyone,

just as the sun shines on everyone.

*Y*ou are the Light. Move to the Divine.

Look through the eyes of the Master, and you

will see what is there for you.

*T*he presence of divine love within
the Master will stir the presence
of divine love within you.

*Y*ou can start finding your own divine love when you start loving others. But that doesn't count until you can love yourself.

$\mathcal{T}$he most precious gift is the gift of self.

The most precious return is the self returning.

*L*oving can cure all.

$\mathcal{L}$oving is action, manifestation, movement,

the consciousness of giving.

$\mathcal{W}$hen you sing from the center of your

beingness, you sing a celestial song.

*T*he Light of the Soul emanates from
the center of your being as living love.
The Soul is noninflictive by nature;
the Soul is joyful. The Soul is a divine river
from the infinite Ocean of Love and Mercy.

*B*efore you express the power of love,

you must first be silent in order to find

out what love is.

When you love, you live. When you live,
God pours forth his energies through
you into the world.

*T*he holy land is wherever divine love is being

made manifest. Wherever you demonstrate

the consciousness of love, that land

becomes sacred and holy.

*H*ome is where the Spirit of Christ reigns eternally, and that is within the loving heart.

The Light of the heart, the Light of the Soul,

the Light of the Christ, the Light of God.

These things are in all.

*T*he spiritual things are the invisible things,

and they will endure forever.

Not one soul is going to be lost.

*Y*ou dwell always in the heart of God.

*L*iving In God's Holy Thoughts

God resides in the kingdom of heaven,

and heaven is right here and now.

*T*he One we are waiting for and the One we have been looking for is already here, and has been here for a long time. You are the spiritual being you've been searching to find.

*T*here will come a time in the Soul of
everyone on this planet when they will receive
the divine Light, and know it.

*T*he name of the game is your willingness

to participate in your life.

$\mathcal{T}$here is a guide inside you, a great counselor, a guiding Light. God is present, working in you as you, pulling your consciousness away from the distractions of the world and back into awareness of Spirit.

*I*t is possible for you to lift out of your
present level of consciousness into
higher levels of consciousness.

Thinking about something doesn't get it done. Feeling about it doesn't get it done. Fantasizing about something doesn't do it. Doing does it.

*W*hen you can allow people to express
their Light their own way, to fulfill their destiny
and walk the path to the drummer they hear,
then you are, in essence, doing the same thing
God does—allowing them the freedom
of their own expression.

*A*ll that you want to be, you already are.
All you have to do is move your awareness there
and recognize the reality of your own Soul.

*I*ntegrity is an indicator in the physical

world of spirituality.

γou were put here with something special

inside you: the ability to contact Spirit within.

$\mathcal{Y}$our job is to awaken to the levels inside you
that are asleep, to awaken to the consciousness
of love, Light, and Sound.

$\mathcal{W}$hen you're living in the now, you can accomplish much more than when you try to live in the past or the future.

Love God with all your heart. Love yourself
with the same devotion. Love all who come
to you as you love God.

Spirituality is the most natural expression in the world. It is your true and abiding nature.

There is nowhere you can go that you're not in the body of God—nowhere. There is no place that you can imagine that you're not within this frequency of Spirit. Even in your darkest moment, you are still in the body of God, a portion of Spirit.

You have a responsibility to be loving.

$\mathcal{W}$isdom is using those things that work for you, for as long as they work for you, and letting go of the things that are not working for you.

*T*hose who sit quietly in the silence that roars the name of the Lord and do the most mundane jobs in love and devotion are performing a beautiful service that God sees as very great, indeed.

$\mathcal{B}$y practicing the song of love,

which is the spiritual exercises, you awaken

to that which you truly are.

*T*o discern Spirit, you must attune yourself
to Spirit and to those who know Spirit.

*T*here's only one key. There's really only one
law—and that is the law of loving.

$\mathcal{L}$oving is the only channel for

clear communication.

*T*he family is the foundation of society.

Love is the foundation of the family.

God is the foundation of love.

*A*ll of your relationships are inside of you.
Ultimately, each relationship you have
with another person reflects
your relationship with yourself.

Your primary relationship is to your own Soul.
If that's clear, then everything else will follow.

*H*ow do you handle fear, insecurity, and anger when they come into your consciousness? Go into the theater of your mind and envision yourself being able to think and plan intelligently.

$\mathcal{J}$ust sit there with the loving process
inside of you because the reward of a loving,
open heart is exactly that.

*F*eelings of discouragement and despair

can come in when you are not realizing

who you really are.

$\mathcal{A}$s you create expectations of people or situations, as you create opinions of what should or should not be taking place with yourself and others, you create your dilemmas.

*D*on't be afraid to be who you are.

Allow yourself the dignity of your own loving.

The thing you've done that you think is so terrible that you must hide it from the world is not unique or special to you. The Inner Master knows those innermost secrets and loves you totally. These things are the "tiddlywinks" of the lower realms. They mean little in Spirit.

*T*he more purity you can perceive,

the more you can add to the glory of the

Light you manifest.

*I*f you want to be an optimist, if you want your

energies to be lifting, if you want to realize

your highest potential for joy and fulfillment,

then you must pledge to yourself that from

this moment, you will become more and more

aware of what you are doing now.

$\mathcal{Y}$ou are greater than any problem, and you have the keys to solve all problems.

*I*n reality you don't win or lose in life's games.
The process is one of completion and
fulfillment, of mastering and thereby lifting
into higher realms of consciousness.

*B*ring your consciousness into line with the

true idea of service by serving with love and joy.

*I*t's important to do whatever is necessary to overcome your obstacles. You can live on faith and belief, but they are not substitutes for mastering, for developing the ability to accomplish.

If you seek the kingdom of heaven,

you're going to find it; if you don't seek it,

you are going to find it, anyway. It's just

going to take a little longer.

We are all extensions of God, and being

extensions, we are all God expressing

on some level.

*R*egardless of what happens, you always
keep going on to the next thing. If you're in an
illusion, go through it. If you're in truth,
go on to greater truths.

*T*here is only one consciousness, and that is

the consciousness of God.

*T*he object in life's game isn't
necessarily to win, but to master the game
and to lift beyond it.

*C*hoose wisely those with whom you are going to associate. Choose those people who are looking in the direction you want to go. Spend your time with people who are also keeping their eyes on the Lord.

*T*he physical body is only one expression of you;
you also express on many other levels.

You have a true self which you may not always
be aware of. The true self is the divine spark
within, the Soul, that which you really are.

You may not know what the Soul is; you may be unable to define it or label it, but you *are* it. Your essence is Soul.

$\mathcal{W}$hen you can approach every experience openly, honestly, and lovingly, maintaining your center and saying, "I know all things are for my learning and upliftment," then you can work through all possibilities. You may also choose not to experience something because you are free in your consciousness and expression.

*I*n your freedom, exercise wisdom.
Hold back from demonstrating your realization,
and allow other people to rise to
theirs naturally, in their own timing.

$\mathcal{W}$hen something works for you, use it.
If you find that it doesn't work, or when
something that used to work stops working
for you, have the wit to drop it.

$\mathcal{Y}$ou're never given anything you can't handle.

Once I said, "But how about this?"

They said, "You still exist." I said, "Yes."

They said, "Then you handled it." God will

never give you anything he can't handle.

$\mathcal{D}$epending upon how you direct your consciousness, you can use anything that comes to you as a stumbling block or as a stepping-stone. You can use everything to your advancement when you see it with a positive consciousness.

*D*epression is a false image. The true self,

the true image, the Soul, is positive.

It is the Spirit within as an extension of

the supreme God. The Soul is perfect.

It represents joy, love, and harmony.

God didn't put you on earth to be a beggar.
He gave you everything you will ever need.

*Y*ou are not a beggar unless you choose to express that consciousness. You have free choices. However you will it, you will have it.

$\mathcal{A}$s you give, you receive.

If you give a lot, you receive a lot. If you give

a little, that's all you get.

You may be alone physically, but you are never alone spiritually. When you reach into the higher levels of consciousness, into the positive areas of Spirit, you have knowledge of your oneness with everything and everyone. There is no separation.

You are already spiritual. You don't have
to try to be what you already are.

*F*ulfilling the prophecies of Jesus is easy,
for when you direct yourself toward the
expression of the Christ, you have the Christ
Consciousness on your side.

*R*ealize that everything is yours and that
you can't use it all at once. Your supply
is always here. It always has been,
it is now, and it always will be.

*W*hen people say things meant to hurt or anger you, you don't have to fight them. You don't have to do anything. Let them have their fun. You simply direct yourself into the consciousness that you want to have.

*Y*ou can have all knowledge. You may not

consciously know everything at one time,

but whatever you direct your attention to,

you can know.

No one can be God, but we can all be coworkers. You cannot become God, but you can become one with God. We stand as One, while maintaining our individuality. All you have to do is assume this consciousness. The law of assumption is a spiritual law, and you will have God consciousness if you start assuming it.

$\mathcal{A}$s you call in the Light, work with the Light, and start assuming that you are the Light, you become the Light.

You can use everything for your advancement if you use it with a positive consciousness.

No one can create an illusion for you
but you, and no one can free you from
an illusion but you.

*M*ake every expression a training ground,

not an end in itself.

*H*old positive images in your mind.

*R*ealize your true self;

that's all that is necessary.

*D*esire (even desire for God) produces resistance, and resistance blocks the process of Soul Transcendence. There is no resistance in the consciousness of God. There is only flow.

$\mathcal{L}$et go and be what you are—a divine being
working here to express a greater degree of
creative and loving consciousness.

When you release your desire for something, your unhappiness goes. When you release the concern about what somebody else thinks about something, your concern about it goes. As you realize that you can't handle other people's lives, your worry about them goes. And when you realize that you can handle your life, your happiness increases.

Sacrifice your desires. When they are gone,

all that is left is your true beingness,

which is everything and nothing.

*P*lace things in the Light to be

balanced and cleared.

$\mathcal{T}$he Light is wonderful; you're wonderful, too, because you have the wit to look at an area and say, "This causes me trouble." It takes courage to walk away from the familiar thing that is not working for you, into the unfamiliar thing wherein you may find your eternal happiness.

*H*appiness is a neutral territory where you have no desires. You have no highs, no lows. You have a high point, but it continues on. You don't talk about highs or lows. You talk about eternal progression. And in the silence that roars the name of the Light and Sound of God, you move on in great tranquility.

*I*t's your attitude toward what you are doing that counts; not just what you are doing, but your attitude toward it.

*D*esire is not what the heart wants. The heart wants a contentment, a peacefulness, a quality of flowing through life like a stream that flows on its path to the ocean. You're flowing on the stream of Light and Sound, into this great ocean of love. You can't get off. You can go a long way to the periphery, but you still keep moving forward. And everyone is going to make it back to the ocean, back into the heart of God.

$\mathcal{L}$iving love means that your love extends unconditionally to all beings. You love everything and everyone present, no exceptions.

*E*ach time you can look into an area of
your unhappiness and see how it can be
changed, you come closer to the
realization of your divinity.

Only the love matters, the pure love,

the unconditional love that is simply

present as God's beingness.

Once you recognize the God essence within

you and within everyone, you can move

through life in a more neutral state.

$\mathcal{B}$e happy and free in your relationship

to yourself.

$\mathcal{T}$he best approach is simply to live in the now, do the best you can with present abilities and talents, and let your actions speak for themselves. That takes understanding and awareness. It also takes love and respect for self. With it comes freedom, a sense of self-worth, and an inner security and serenity that is worth everything.

*T*he consciousness of love can cure anything.

Spiritual progression is a continual process of leaving behind the old, familiar patterns and venturing into the new.

$\mathcal{A}$s you realize that there is no reason to hide what is true for you, you find yourself living a life of integrity, a life of loving. In so doing, you open yourself to an inner experience of loving and freedom that transcends words.

Go inward for your happiness and fulfillment.

*D*iscover where you can assist, rather than interfere. Assistance is a very beautiful form of loving.

*D*on't try to control people. Just let them unfold the way they want. It's beautiful to sit with others and have them start telling you about themselves. The support is in listening and hearing them reveal themselves to you a little bit at a time, while you remain free of judgments or preconceived opinions about what they should or shouldn't be.

*T*he person who understands you the most, who cares for you the most, who can do the most for you is *you*. The ultimate relationship is with yourself, and it's important to keep that inner relationship harmonious. To do that, you have to be in a continual state of self-education, and you need to tune in to the source of who you really are.

γou were given life to experience abundance and joy, and if you're not experiencing that, look at what you're doing to block yourself. Then use that block as a stepping stone. Don't get rid of it; instead, use it—and everything—as an opportunity to lift yourself.

When you give of your ability, your joy, your gifts and your creativity, people coming behind you (whom you may or may not know) are able to partake of the blessings you extend.

*I*t is by your actions that you are known.

Love awakens you. That love is what we're here for—to love each other, to be with each other, to live in spiritual communion.

*I*f you start feeling tired, ask yourself if you are doing your work or the work of the Lord. Ask yourself if you are a taker. Ask if you are fighting, trying to get a hold of something that is not yours and never will be. Once you start getting answers to those questions, you'll say, "Oh, forget the taking, I'll just give of the overflow."

*I*t is time to come back into your heart, into that

one place that is the essence of who you are,

into that one place that continually vibrates,

"I am love."

*I*t is time to stand forward in the integrity of who you are and to celebrate the love and joy that is inside you. It is time to reach out and touch to others, to share your love, to uplift those next to you. By doing that, you'll make this world a better place in which to live.

$\mathcal{W}$hen you get sick and tired of being tired

and sick—you'll change.

*B*ecome aware of the divine presence that lives within you, as you, and use this awareness as your springboard into higher consciousness.

*T*he ultimate goal is union with God.

*T*he difference between man and God is that man can kiss you on the outside, but God kisses you on the inside.

*T*he price of freedom is eternal vigilance.

*Y*ou are the Light. You are divine. You are in a state of becoming what you already are.

*I*t takes great courage to see the face of God because you have to stop wanting, you have to let go of all desire patterns, and accept what is.

*Y*ou cannot allow anything discourteous to get into your mental attitude toward anything or anyone, including yourself. The instant you do, your relationship goes out of balance. There is no emotionalism, no sentimentality, no wishful thinking in all of this. You simply realize that if you identify anything as either intelligent or unintelligent, good or bad, friendly or unfriendly, cooperative or uncooperative, that is precisely how it will appear—for all you experience is the state of your own consciousness being made manifest in your outward experience.

*A*ll living things are individual instruments
through which Spirit thinks, speaks, acts,
and reveals Itself. We are all interrelated in a
common accord, a common purpose, and
a common good. We are members of a vast
cosmic orchestra in which each living instrument
is essential to the complementary and
harmonious playing of the whole.

*T*he mind is to be used today. It's an instrument of perception. The emotions are to be released from yesterday and used today. They're instruments for feeling. The mind and emotions are tools for perception, feeling, and action. These bring completion on this level.

*Y*ou can be honest and true to yourself without

making anyone else wrong.

*G*o into situations with what you want to find there. If you want to find Spirit everywhere you go, take it with you.

*T*urn the Light of your consciousness on

yourself and bring yourself awake.

$\mathcal{T}$he Traveler is a special aspect of the Holy
Spirit. You don't give yourself over to the force
that is the Traveler; you *are* it. It is the guiding
Light. It is your own inner guidance.

*A*ll you have to do is be the Light and assist anyone who comes to you. It's like saying three magic words: "God bless you." Then each person rises to the challenge of their own true self, their own Soul, their own God consciousness within.

*A*cceptance is one of the primary laws of
Spirit and one of the most important laws in
spiritual unfoldment. On the impersonal level,
you accept everything that is going on. On the
personal level, you select what you bring in to
form your life and your moral and spiritual
values, and to support your true quest. You select
those things that will work for your highest
good and your best expression.

*A*ccept your mistakes, accept your actions,
accept every situation as a learning experience
and as a stepping-stone. As you
accept yourself and your own expression,
you are really on your way.

*T*o support yourself in the Light consciousness,

it's important to be around and attuned to those

people who are also in a Light consciousness,

or who are moving in that direction.

There are many people who are expressing

a Light consciousness.

$\mathcal{Y}$ou are always in your own movement of
spiritual inner awareness. You can come together
with other people to assist each other
as part of this movement.

Your questions, your doubts, and your fears are
not living love. Do everything in God's name,
and you will be walking straight toward God.

God's name is living love. If, every morning, you say, "Here I come, Lord; open your arms," you may find the love of your life awaiting you.

But you must bring your living love present.

*M*anifest living love.

Living love is loving yourself first, so that you can love others. It's taking care of yourself, so that you can help take care of others. It's doing those things that are good for you, so that you'll be happy, healthy, and a joy to be with.

*I*f you shower and change and put on your best
cologne so you'll smell good for your husband or
wife, you're doing things backward. It's when
you smell good for yourself that you are
manifesting living love. You are clean
for yourself, for the Spirit that resides
within your bodily temple.

iving love is the service of the moment. To
reach the Traveler Consciousness, you must
manifest living love. You must consistently give
in living service. You don't give for the reward
of giving. You give because it is love's nature
to give. You do the right thing just because
it is the right thing to do.

$\mathcal{E}$xpress lovingly toward everyone

you encounter.

*B*ecome God's faithful servant, experiencing
the joy that comes with serving unconditionally.
You will be able to do anything that is needed in
the moment, knowing that service done in love
is the highest expression on the physical level.

$\mathcal{F}$orgive yourself.

*F*ind the center within and let your wisdom come forward from that point. Learn to work from a selfless nature. Put aside this world, and do for the other person in a total love of doing.

*U*se each experience to awaken yourself.

*A*ll that really matters is that you know you're living and breathing, that you are a student, and that you are becoming a better student all the time. I'm not necessarily talking about becoming a better student on the outer levels; I'm talking about *you*, that part of you behind your eyes. I'm talking about the *you* who is awakening to your greater self, to your divine self within.

$\mathcal{B}$e where you are and be who you are—

honestly, openly, purely.

*I*f you can stop for a moment in your thinking
and your questing and listen to the silence, you
may start becoming aware of many levels of
consciousness. You may become aware that you
are on all levels of Light simultaneously.
The trick is to learn to shift your awareness
to where you wish to be.

*I*t is important to take time for yourself each day—time to focus into your spiritual awareness, time to drop the physical concerns of the moment and once again become aware that you are spiritual, that you are divine, that you are, through your Soul, an extension of the supreme God.

*M*ove through all the experiences
that come to you.

*R*each out and embrace the Traveler in your inner awareness. Know that form as the essence of yourself, your Inner Master, which is closer to you than your breath, more real than any other level. Know that in the Traveler's love, you are walking straight into the heart of God, and awaken to the pure form of God's beingness.

*T*urn to your inner Light.

*D*on't judge your inner or outer process.
Let it be whatever it is. Use each experience to
awaken yourself to the greatest degree possible.
Use each experience as an opportunity to
work with the Light and to exercise the
Christ Consciousness within.

*U*se your spiritual exercise time to experience "now" as the pure and perfect moment that it is. If you are concerned about a mistake you made at work, forget it in the moment of your spiritual exercises. It is not now. If you are concerned about your relationship with your spouse or lover, let it go. Sacrifice your concern and use the energy that you would have put into worrying to lift higher in the Spirit.

*K*eep forgiveness and unconditional

love flowing.

$\mathcal{B}$e very selfish about getting to your next level of spiritual unfoldment. Love everybody, no matter what. Love yourself, no matter what.

Present yourself daily to the Spirit. Make yourself available. Come into Spirit's presence.

*A*rise to the consciousness of the

Christ within you.

When you have found the almighty power within, which is the consciousness of Soul, that power will transcend the world because it is the power of the supreme generator of Light and love. It is not reflected power, existing only in reflection. It is the power of knowing, the power of being. It *is*.

*U*se every opportunity to grow in wisdom,

understanding, and empathy.

Realize that there is a great wind that blows
from heaven and that this wind is Light and
Sound. In this stream of Light and Sound,
you can dance all the way across the universes.
You can turn your consciousness into it,
and know that you and the Light are one.
You can know that you are divine.

*W*hatever your relationship with other people—lover, spouse, friend, colleague, parent, etc.—use your Light consciousness to lift them. When you bring forward the consciousness of Light through *actions* (not necessarily through words), you'll find them lifting.

*W*hen spiritual love is expressed between people, the greatest commandment that has been placed on the planet is being fulfilled. This commandment is to love the Lord thy God with all thy heart and with all thy mind and with all thy Soul, and to love your neighbor as yourself. God resides in everyone. So as you love the least one and the greatest one equally, you are fulfilling God's commandment to love Him.

As you love unconditionally, you love God,
you love Spirit, and you experience a
perpetual upliftment.

$\mathcal{L}$ove without condition, without strings. The only strings are your devotion to the Light, to God, to Spirit, to the awareness of Self.

$\mathcal{L}$ove may not be looking at another person,

not even at your beloved. Love is

looking toward the same goals.

*T*he answers to the questions you have are

inside of you already.

*I*f it's done in love, it will work.

*I*t's important to remember that there are really

no crises or emergencies.

*W*hen you allow your mind to become calm,

your emotions can stabilize.

Love sees through to the heart. Eyes see

the surface. The eyes feel betrayed,

but the heart fulfills itself.

When things are made new in your heart, you start to feel wonderful about life. You get up with an attitude of, "Good morning, God," instead of, "Oh, God... morning." You are actually excited to get out of bed and meet the day that God has created for you, and you rush right out into it.

$\mathcal{Y}$our experience of Spirit will allow you to claim authority over your life and your consciousness. It is the only authority that counts for anything.

$\mathcal{L}$ove is present all the time, just as Spirit is around all the time. Love provides the cohesiveness for every aspect of the universe. Without loving, things would disintegrate; there would be no form through which anything could be expressed. Sometimes the loving is expressed in ways that are pleasing to you, and sometimes in ways that are not so pleasing or that are misunderstood, but the love is always there.

Nothing here is designed to hurt or harm you. It is all for you to use to lift yourself into Spirit. It all points you toward God. It is all for your benefit.

God may be using your family, friends, boss, or even total strangers to bring discipline to you, but it is really coming from Spirit. Spirit loves you enough to point up to you the mistakes you are making and to assist you in correcting them. When you can see the loving *in* every action and *behind* every action, you are on your way to seeing God in everyone. You can see the God in everyone and still recognize the mistakes of this level and the areas that need improvement. The two are not mutually exclusive; they coexist.

*T*he Soul, the Spirit within, is perfect and is

an extension of God into this level. The

consciousness on this level is continuously

progressing. If you can awaken to the dual

nature of yourself and others, you are awakening

to Spirit in greater reality.

$\mathcal{E}$nter into the warmth and graciousness of God within you. Go inside to Spirit, to God, to your own loving nature. Don't go inside and look at your emotions, or all you'll see is upset. Don't go inside and look at your mind; it will keep pushing you back out here, and you'll never see anything else. Go past those levels and you'll start moving into some of the most glorious territories that have yet to be investigated.

See the loving in every action and

behind every action.

*O*ver and over again, we come back to the same thing: spiritual exercises are the key to your freedom. It is through the inner process that you will gain the knowledge, wisdom, strength, and clarity to lift out of these worldly levels and move into Spirit. It is the most important skill you can develop here.

*D*o whatever it takes to assume

responsibility for yourself.

Life is awareness, awareness is life. The degree of your awareness is the degree of your loving. The greater your awareness, the greater your loving. The more you open to Spirit, the more clearly you see and the more completely you love. When you become one with Spirit, there is no separation from anything or anyone. There is only loving of one thing—your divine self, the God that is you and that is also everyone and everything else.

The spiritual energy brings liberation, and liberation is the keynote of the Soul. Liberation is the inner attitude of freedom. It is not what you do; it is how you do it. You can say right now, "I am free from the shackles of my emotional habits. I am free from the addictions of my mind. I am living a life of preference."

Gain the experience of Spirit for yourself. Don't substitute anyone else's experience for your own. Don't let anyone else interpret Spirit for you. Look to your own experience and interpret your own experience. You do not need others to tell you what your experience is. No one else can ever truly know, and that includes your family and friends as well as psychics and fortune-tellers.

*G*ive of the goodness that you are. Give of the truth that you are. Give of the Spirit that you are. The reward will be that you know those aspects of yourself more deeply and truly. The Spirit will become more alive and present for you in every moment, and you will walk hand in hand with the Beloved and know yourself and God as one.

$\int$ee the God in everyone.

$\mathcal{E}$nter into all situations and relationships in a

state of love, freedom, and responsibility.

You will find life flows more easily for you.

$\mathcal{T}$he Soul is the essence of Light and love and Sound, and those are the essences that stir you continually. Soul brings joy. As you express the essence of Soul, you demonstrate divine love.

Come into the process of understanding and maintain your calm by *consciously, directly holding,* not letting flights of fancy take you where they will. Come back to this moment, continually, and you'll find that tensions disappear, distractions disappear, and you'll start coming into the calmness of right now.

*K*eep order within yourself.

*T*hose who realize God consciousness are those who enter into it, hold to it, and maintain it as the one thing they must always remember.

*G*od lives inside of you as you, and your body
is the temple in which resides the
magnificence of God.

When you find yourself getting upset because of what someone else does or says to you and you feel like your toes have been stomped on, pull your emotions back in. Place your loyalty once again with your Soul, with your spiritual exercises, with the upliftment of your consciousness. Focus on the unconditional loving you know you can experience and express.

$\mathcal{W}$hen you find truth in any situation,
you are discovering God. When you do not seek
to manipulate what presents itself to you,
but accept and deal with what is, you are
tapping into Spirit.

$\mathcal{A}$t times, we can all express loving in ways
that aren't necessarily appreciated. But if you can
realize that loving is the essential message in all
your communication, you'll be further ahead.

$\mathcal{T}$he mind is not necessarily a tool for under-

standing. It's a tool for gathering information.

The spiritual heart is the tool for understanding.

And the Soul is the tool for truth.

When I say it takes great courage to see the face of God, it's because you have to see the face of God in all people. That does take a lot of courage because you have to continually move yourself past your personality, prejudices, and points of view, until you recognize your oneness with all other personalities.

Sometimes doing nothing is the greatest gift you can give to another. Sometimes just your presence is the greatest gift.

*D*on't create separation by looking at physical bodies as being "there." Look at them as being "here." Look on them as being manifestations of truth, God, and Spirit, all carrying the same essence as yours. Then you can love them all.

You can keep the awareness of the Light and
of God present in your heart, no matter what.
When you do, you stand as a beacon of
Light for everyone around you.

$\mathcal{W}$e all need reference points. We all want
to see where we're going. When you are
loyal to yourself, you can develop
inner reference points of peace,
contentment, and a sense of worthiness.

*A*ll you have to do is turn inside to find that the Traveler never goes away. It's always with you. It's always present. It's always there for you.

When the Soul is present, you experience love and joy in all that you do. You are like a little kid, singing and playing your way through all sorts of situations.

$\mathcal{L}$ove can appear in all sorts of forms. It can appear as discipline. It can appear as limitation. It can appear as freedom. It doesn't have just one expression.

You are in God's hands.

*P*ut your loyalty to the Soul and to your awareness of Soul, right here and now.

$\mathcal{B}$ring joy present in your life at
every moment, regardless of what
is going on around you.

*B*e loyal to your next breath. That type of loyalty will lead you to seeing the face of God.

$\mathcal{B}$e loyal to your own well-being and happiness. If you go through an unhappy period, remain loyal to your own happiness, and you'll find yourself returning to happiness. Be loyal to your own upliftment so that if you get a little down or depressed, you'll just move through it and come right back around to being happy and uplifted. Be loyal to doing spiritual exercises. If you miss a day or two, your loyalty to doing them will reassert itself and you'll move back into the process.

$\mathcal{M}$ake it a habit to be loyal to the activities that serve the highest part of you and to the attitudes that bring you joy and happiness.

*F*ocus on love, the divine love. It can increase circulation, increase oxygen supply, increase vitality. You can feel great—dis-ease disappears.

$\mathcal{B}$e loyal to the loving inside you for yourself
and for others.

Nurture those parts of your expression which are positive. When you are living from a positive consciousness, you cannot be hurt. When you are loving, nothing can harm you.

*B*laze a path inside you which leads to love and joy. Foster and nurture all the positive aspects of yourself. Dwell on that which is good.

Strengthen the good things about yourself.
Let them become your habits, so that in quiet
moments, it is the positive expressions
that come naturally to you.

When you experience the loving within you
and allow others in so they can experience your
loving, you find your love growing.

Use all the tools you have to live your life in
the most effective and joyful way available to you.

*T*ruth is everywhere.

$\mathcal{L}$oving is the most important quality you can

nurture in yourself.

When you are loyal to yourself, you can develop inner reference points of peace, contentment, and a sense of worthiness.

You may have to disturb yourself in order to become aware of yourself and establish a reference point for your progress. Then you can know that you are forever moving upward in your spiritual progression into the heart of God.

You're in the physical body, but you are not it.
You are on the planet, but you are not the planet.
It's a truth and a paradox that everything you
are to become, you are right now.

One of the things you do not have to do is
seek love. You are love already. If you were not,
you would not be here.

*I*f God is on your side, who can be against you?

*I*t matters little what someone else does or has done. What matters is what you're doing right now.

*I*f you stay focused in the now, you can have tremendous joy and great fun wherever you find yourself. It's all your attitude, and your attitude is your choice.

*T*here are at least two ways you can go through this life: you can go through crying or you can go through laughing. It's your choice.

When you can keep a positive attitude, you can learn from any situation. You can continually be growing and lifting in consciousness and awareness, and life can really be a beautiful experience.

$\mathcal{T}$he Light of your own consciousness is the most magnificent gift you can ever give, it is the most valuable thing there is. Your individual expression of the Light is so precious in its perfection and beauty.

One of the greatest ways to break up
crystallizations is laughter. Laughter expresses
great joy and brings everyone to a common
ground of oneness.

See your experience through the eyes of

the Master.

*W*ithin every illusion, there is some truth.

*R*ecognize the divine Soul within

every person you meet.

γou are in the process of discovering your

Beloved, your Soul.

*T*he world is your illusionary field.

Your Soul is your reality.

*W*ithin everything physical and finite, there
is infinite Spirit.

One way to get back on the spiritual path

is to be honest.

One of the first signs that you are moving from your spiritual path is the expression of gossip.

When in doubt, you just don't do; you hold until you see your direction more clearly.

*T*he way has already been prepared for you.

All you have to do is walk it.

*A*waken your will. When you decide to do it is your choice. Spirit does not push.

*A*ll you have to do is move forward and

claim your divine inheritance.

$\mathcal{Y}$ou are here to gain knowledge of all the

levels of creation.

$\mathcal{W}$hy bow down and worship a little piece of green paper with a fancy design on it when you can have God and the Light and the love and the energy of Spirit to sustain you?

*R*emember that you are a creator and that
which you create you must fulfill.

$\mathcal{L}$ift and secure yourself first before you

attempt to lift anyone else.

*U*ltimately, your only judge is you.

γou cannot be shut off from God—you can only

think you are.

*G*od is everywhere, in all things and in all levels of consciousness. Things that appear to be negative are only learning devices, not punishments.

*T*here is nothing to control. There is only

a state of being.

*W*hen Spirit radiates down, you come to the point where you realize, "My God and I are one."

*T*he first law of Spirit is acceptance.

$\int$elf-awareness is a state of movement—

awareness is activity.

God does not forsake you;

you forsake yourself.

*T*he loving nature is the key to all things. When you speak, do not speak out of a level of hurt or a level of lack. Speak out of a level of fulfillment, out of your loving nature.

*T*he wind that blows from heaven is the Light of God, and that is what we call the Christ.

*T*he Christ within you knows the Christ in others. To many people, the Christ has not appeared yet. To others, he has come and gone. But those who dwell in it know the Christ is eternally present.

*A*s you come to understand that Christ
is not the man, that man is of Christ,
you start unfolding.

$\mathcal{W}$hen you sing in your dreams, that is the

language of the Soul.

*E*very Soul has the divine message
within itself.

*C*hrist-mass, or Christmas, is not the exchanging of a gift out there, but a receiving of the gift of the Christ into you.

$\mathcal{P}$rayer is talking to God. Meditation is listening for the answer. Contemplation is looking at the path to God. Spiritual exercises are walking the path to God.

*G*od meets you at the point of your action.

*I*t is the heart that does the work. Listen to the heart. It will tell you truly where you live. When you turn to your heart, which the Light has filled to overflowing, you may know the joy of the Soul.

$\mathcal{T}$he kingdom of heaven is within, and therein resides the Beloved.

*Y*ou are the Beloved.

*W*hat you can behold, you can become.

ABOUT THE AUTHOR

A TEACHER AND LECTURER of international stature, with millions of books in print, John-Roger is a luminary in the lives of thousands of people. For over three decades, his wisdom, humor, common sense and love have helped people to discover the Spirit within themselves and find health, peace, and prosperity.

With two co-authored books on the *New York Times* Bestseller List to his credit, and more than three dozen spiritual and self-help books and audio albums, John-Roger offers extraordinary insights on a wide range of topics. He is the founder of the nondenominational Church of the Movement of Spiritual Inner Awareness (MSIA) which focuses on Soul Transcendence; President of the Institute for Individual and World Peace; Chancellor of the University of Santa Monica; President of Peace Theological Seminary and College of Philosophy; and founder of Insight Transformational Seminars.

John-Roger has given over 5,000 seminars worldwide, many of which are televised nationally on his cable program, "That Which Is," through the Network of Wisdoms. He has been a featured guest on "Larry King Live," "Politically Incorrect," "The Roseanne Show," and appears regularly on radio and television.

An educator and minister by profession, John-Roger continues to transform the lives of many, by educating them in the wisdom of the spiritual heart.

If you've enjoyed this book, you may want to explore the following resources through the Movement of Spiritual Inner Awareness, where John-Roger serves as Spiritual Advisor:

Soul Awareness Discourses—
A Home Study Course for Your Spiritual Growth

The heart of John-Roger's teachings, Soul Awareness Discourses provide a structured and methodical approach to gaining greater awareness of ourselves and our relationship to the world and to God. Each year's study course contains twelve lessons, one for each month. Discourses offer a wealth of practical keys to more successful living. Even more, they provide keys to greater spiritual knowledge and awareness of the Soul.

$100 one-year subscription

To order call MSIA at 323-737-4055

Soul Awareness Tape (SAT) Series

These audio tapes provide a new talk by John-Roger every month on a variety of topics, ranging from practical living to spiritual upliftment.

In addition, SAT subscribers may purchase previous SAT releases.

$100 one-year subscription

To order call MSIA at 323-737-4055

Loving Each Day Subscription

Loving Each Day quotes are offered in the form of a daily e-mail message from MSIA that contains an uplifting quote or passage from John Morton or John-Roger, intended to inspire the reader to reflect on the Spirit within. *Loving Each Day* is available in four languages—English, Spanish, French and Portuguese.

A subscription is free upon request.

To subscribe, please visit the web site, www.msia.org.

Spiritual Warrior: The Art of Spiritual Living

By John-Roger

This book is essential for every person who wants to integrate his or her spiritual and material lives and make them both work. A practical guide to finding greater meaning in everyday life, this book is a #1 *Los Angeles Times* Healthy Bestseller.

$20, hardbound

ISBN 0-914829-36-X

Available in bookstores everywhere or from MSIA at 323-737-4055.

www.spiritualwarrior.org

We welcome your comments and questions.

MSIA

P.O. Box 513935

Los Angeles, CA 90051-1935

323-737-4055

soul@msia.org

www.msia.org